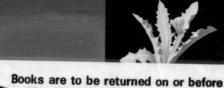

The World of Weather

CONTENTS

Breath of life

Starry Night over the Rhône, Vincent van Gogh, 1888. As the light from stars travels towards us, belts of warm and cold air in the atmosphere make it twinkle.

From our first cry to our dying gasp, we are sustained by the air about us. The air contains a **gas** called **oxygen**, which is essential to animal life – we would be dead within minutes without it – and we take oxygen into our bodies each time we breathe in. Plants would not survive without another gas. They need **carbon dioxide** to make food in their leaves. The air surrounds the Earth in a deep layer called the **atmosphere**. This stretches about 700 kilometres out into space, but compared to the Earth's size it is about as thick as the skin on a peach. There is no air out in space, which is why astronauts have to wear oxygen packs when they leave their spacecraft.

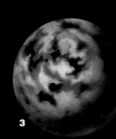

1. Earth was born about 4.6 billion years ago. Soon after, it was a ball of blazing rock and gases.

2. As Earth cooled, its surface hardened into a crust (♦) and an atmosphere formed.

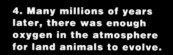

3. Water vapour condensed from the atmosphere and fell as rain, creating the oceans where, millions of years later, tiny single-celled plants flourished. Like all plants these gave off oxygen, slowly enriching the atmosphere.

4. Many millions of years later, there was enough oxygen in the atmosphere for land animals to evolve.

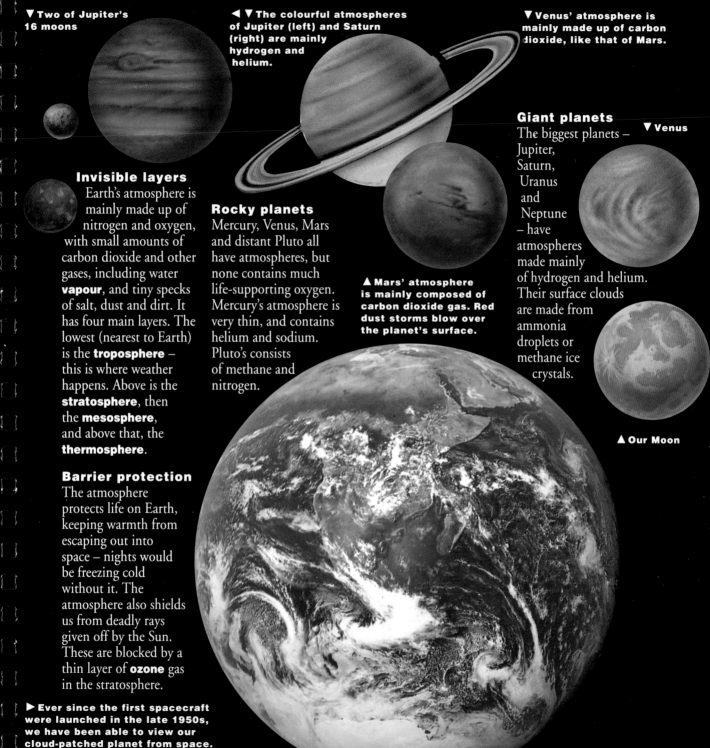

▼ **Two of Jupiter's 16 moons**

◀ ▼ **The colourful atmospheres of Jupiter (left) and Saturn (right) are mainly hydrogen and helium.**

▼ **Venus' atmosphere is mainly made up of carbon dioxide, like that of Mars.**

Invisible layers

Earth's atmosphere is mainly made up of nitrogen and oxygen, with small amounts of carbon dioxide and other gases, including water **vapour**, and tiny specks of salt, dust and dirt. It has four main layers. The lowest (nearest to Earth) is the **troposphere** – this is where weather happens. Above is the **stratosphere**, then the **mesosphere**, and above that, the **thermosphere**.

Rocky planets

Mercury, Venus, Mars and distant Pluto all have atmospheres, but none contains much life-supporting oxygen. Mercury's atmosphere is very thin, and contains helium and sodium. Pluto's consists of methane and nitrogen.

▲ **Mars' atmosphere is mainly composed of carbon dioxide gas. Red dust storms blow over the planet's surface.**

Giant planets

The biggest planets – Jupiter, Saturn, Uranus and Neptune – have atmospheres made mainly of hydrogen and helium. Their surface clouds are made from ammonia droplets or methane ice crystals.

▼ **Venus**

▲ **Our Moon**

Barrier protection

The atmosphere protects life on Earth, keeping warmth from escaping out into space – nights would be freezing cold without it. The atmosphere also shields us from deadly rays given off by the Sun. These are blocked by a thin layer of **ozone** gas in the stratosphere.

▶ **Ever since the first spacecraft were launched in the late 1950s, we have been able to view our cloud-patched planet from space.**

Something in the air

In 1774, the English chemist Joseph Priestley found that something in the air is essential to animal life. Today we know it as the gas oxygen.

We cannot see, touch or taste air, but we can feel it cooling our faces, hear it rustling the leaves, and watch it sweeping clouds across the sky. As long as 2,500 years ago, the Ancient Greeks thought that air is made of something and has weight. But it was not until the 1600s that scientists began to devise instruments to study air. And it was only in the 1770s that the **gases** in air were identified and named.

▼ Oxygen was named by the French chemist Antoine Lavoisier in 1777. Below he is conducting an experiment to prove that we need more oxygen when exercising.

A pump of the 1700s, used to study air pressure.

The scales of fir cones close up when it is damp, and open out when dry weather returns. ◆

Weather forecasting

People soon discovered that air pressure is affected by the weather and began using barometers to help predict it. A high pressure reading on a barometer means that settled, dry weather is likely, while a swift drop to low pressure signals bad weather, with wind, rain and storms.

Nature knows best

Some plants are so sensitive to changes in the weather that they act like natural barometers. A sure sign that rain is on the way is when the scales of pine cones fit together snugly, for example, while the fruits of the scarlet pimpernel break open only in dry, settled weather. Animals give out weather-warning signals, as well. Insects fly lower when rain is coming, because their wings get heavier as the air becomes damper – frogs come out in their hundreds to feast on this low-flying banquet. If you see cockroaches during the day, there is probably a storm brewing.

Weather vanes

Perching seagulls always face into the wind to keep their feathers from ruffling.

Seagull

Thermometers

Plants and animals are very sensitive to temperature. If it drops below 10 °C, dandelion flowers close right up. Colder still, at around 1 °C, rhododendron leaves curl in and droop. In southern Europe, you can be sure the temperature is above 20 °C if cicadas are singing loudly.

Dandelion

Cockroach

Cicada

Scarlet pimpernel fruit

Rhododendron

Red sky at night...

If air is invisible, why is the sky blue? The sky is given its colour by the Sun. Sunlight may look colourless, but it is really a mixture of all the hues of the rainbow. As sunlight travels towards us, it is scattered into its separate colours by the **atmosphere**. Blue light is scattered the most, and becomes the main colour that we see. By the time evening comes, the Sun is low in the sky and farther away from us, so its light has to

pass through more air. The extra dust and water **vapour** in this thicker layer of air mean that red light is now scattered most of all, and we see a beautiful red sunset.

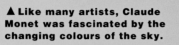

▲ Like many artists, Claude Monet was fascinated by the changing colours of the sky.

1. *Haystacks, Late Summer, Giverny*, 1891.
2. *Haystacks, Noon*, 1890.
3. *Haystacks at Giverny, Sunset*, 1889.

All the colours of the sky

The sky is bluest on clear, cloudless days when the Sun is at its highest, in the middle of the day. In the early morning, the sky is often a honey yellow, while last thing at night it may turn a flaming red.

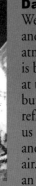

▲ The higher you climb, the thinner the air becomes. With less dust and water to scatter light, the sky gets darker.

Dawn and dusk

We would not see dawn and dusk without the atmosphere. The Sun is below the horizon at these times of day, but some of its light is reflected back towards us by the specks of dust and water floating in the air. If Earth did not have an atmosphere, night would simply snap into day – rather like a great lamp being switched on in the heavens!

Soaking up sunshine

Sunlight has to travel 150 million kilometres through space to reach us. Over half of its heat is bounced back into space by the clouds, but the remainder warms the land and sea, and gives all the energy that green plants need to grow.

Seeing sunbeams

Sunlight is invisible to the human eye. We see sunbeams because the specks of dust and water in the air act like billions of tiny mirrors, reflecting the light.

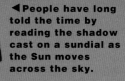

◄ People have long told the time by reading the shadow cast on a sundial as the Sun moves across the sky.

Out of a cloudy sky

On summer days, clouds look like tufts of cottonwool drifting across the sky. But if you could reach up and touch them you would discover that they are not fluffy – they are made of billions of tiny water droplets or ice crystals. All air contains water, and near the ground it is usually in the form of the invisible **gas**, water **vapour**. When air rises, however, it gets colder, and cool air cannot hold as much water vapour as warm air. Some of the vapour now **condenses** into the microscopic water droplets that make clouds. If clouds form high in the sky, where the air is very cold, the vapour condenses into ice crystals.

A climber gazes at a sea of clouds, in this painting by the German artist Caspar David Friedrich (c. 1818).

▶ Clouds have three basic shapes. The highest, called cirrus, are thin and wispy. Cumulus clouds are white, fluffy clumps. While stratus, the lowest, are flat and layered.

▲ High, feathery cirrus clouds, made of ice crystals

▲ Stratocumulus – sheets of rounded cloud

▲ High cirrocumulus

▼ Fluffy cumulus

▼ Altocumulus – small patches of cloud

▼ Stratus – fog-like sheets of low-lying cloud

Naming clouds

Clouds drift across the sky in so many beautiful shapes and colours that it seems impossible to name them all. Yet there are only ten basic kinds of cloud, and three shapes – stratus, cumulus and cirrus. Our system of grouping and naming clouds was devised in 1803, by Luke **Howard**.

Weather watching

Clouds can provide useful clues about the weather. Some mean rain is on its way, others indicate fine settled weather, and yet others are a sure sign of a storm. The different clouds form at various heights in the sky.

Low-lying stratus

Stratus and nimbostratus are the lowest clouds you will see in the sky. Nimbostratus form a thick, grey layer and bring steady rain or snow. Stratus are thick sheets of fog-like cloud which often bring drizzle, but not heavy rain.

Cumulus clouds

Cumulus are the clouds that look most like cottonwool. They form fluffy heaps, and small ones are a sign that good weather is coming. But cumulus often clump together and grow upwards, gaining puffy, cauliflower-shaped heads. If they keep on growing, and get darker, they may turn into cumulonimbus and bring thunder and lightning.

Lumpy and bumpy
Stratocumulus are lumpy sheets of rounded cloud which may bring light falls of rain. Altocumulus look like a jumbled pile of small, greyish-white clouds.

Higher and higher
Altostratus form thin, wispy layers high in the sky, and warn of rain. Cirrocumulus are tiny, high clumps of cloud which indicate that cold weather is on the way.

Hazy and wispy
Cirrus are wispy clouds made of ice crystals, which form above 6,000 metres. Cirrostratus look like a hazy mist and can mean that rain or snow is coming.

Thunderstorms
Cumulonimbus are bigger and darker than cumulus, and bring rain, snow or hail. Sometimes they grow huge – the biggest can tower 15,000 metres up into the sky – and unleash violent thunderstorms!

◀ A bolt of lightning is released by a huge cumulonimbus cloud. Lightning is a giant electrical spark. Air heated by it expands so violently that it creates the great cracking sound we call thunder.

Fold up the page to see
this puffy cumulus cloud
grow into a towering
cumulonimbus storm cloud.

Raining cats...

Shower at Shono, c. 1833, by Hiroshige

Drizzle, shower, downpour, deluge ...

our language is never at a loss for words

to describe it, but what actually causes rain?

Raindrops form inside clouds, as billions of tiny water droplets

bump into each other and combine, forming bigger, heavier

droplets. Eventually, the droplets get so heavy that they can no

longer float in the air, and they start to tumble down through

the clouds. As the droplets fall, they collide with other droplets

and get even larger, until the final raindrop is several thousand

times its original size. Every single raindrop is made up of at least a million of the

original, microscopic cloud droplets!

▲▼ Dew (above) forms on clear, still nights, when water vapour in the air condenses into water droplets. Frost (below) is frozen dew.

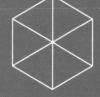

◄ **Hailstones can grow to be huge. The heaviest ever found weighed just over 1 kilogram.**

No two snowflakes have exactly the same pattern, but they are all made from ice crystals with six sides or points. The crystals are tiny, and can only be seen under a microscope.

Hail

Hail forms when droplets at the top of storm clouds freeze. They fall, but are repeatedly flung back to the cloud tops by gusts of air. They keep gathering more coats of ice until they are heavy enough to plummet to the ground.

Freezing rain

If rain falls on really cold days, it freezes instantly on everything it touches. It coats trees, telephone lines, cars and roads with thick layers of clear, smooth ice.

▼ **Ships can only visit Antarctica in summer, when the coastal ice melts and breaks up.**

Snow

When the air in clouds gets very cold, some water **vapour condenses** into tiny ice crystals. Water droplets freeze on to the ice crystals, which grow larger until they fall to the ground as snowflakes. The same vapour that makes 1 millimetre of rain may fall as 10 millimetres of snow.

Ancient snow

Antarctica is so cold that snow rarely melts there. New snow settles on top of the old, pressing it down over time to create great flowing sheets of ice, hundreds of metres thick. In places, the Antarctic ice sheet is up to 4.8 kilometres thick, and over 2 million years old.

A foggy day...

Fog forms in the same way as clouds do, when water **vapour** cools and **condenses** into tiny water droplets. Unlike clouds, though, fog forms just

▲ San Francisco's Golden Gate Bridge is often hidden by sea fog.

above the ground or water and spreads

slowly upwards. As it gets higher, it

thins and disappears – broken

up by the wind and by the

Sun warming the air.

◀ Smog can settle over a city when warm, polluted air is trapped beneath a blanket of colder air.

Smog
The word smog originally described a thick brew of smoky air and fog, but we now also use it for a kind of air **pollution** caused by sunlight reacting with the **gases** given off by cars and factories. Smog can be very unhealthy if it is really thick and heavy.

Fog is very dangerous at sea, so ships use a foghorn to signal their whereabouts to other sea traffic. Early foghorns like this one were driven by a plunger.

All kinds of fog
Because fog can form in different ways, we have various names for it. Ground fog happens inland on nights that are clear and fairly calm. As the soil, plants, rivers and lakes cool, they give off water vapour into the air, where it condenses into tiny water droplets. Frontal fog occurs when warm air passes over a cold layer of air near the ground.

Sea fog and steam fog
Sea fog forms near the coast, when warm, moist air travels over and is cooled by cold land or water. Steam fog, on the other hand, forms when cold air passes over warm water – this may happen out at sea, or over inland lakes and rivers.

We call thin fog 'mist'. It is misty if you can see farther than 1 kilometre. When visibility is less than 1 kilometre, it is foggy.

Tricks of the light

1.+2. Haloes are misty circles around the Moon or Sun caused by light reflecting off ice crystals in high, thin clouds.

1

Deep in the desert, a thirsty traveller gasps to see a shimmering pool of

water … but can he believe his eyes? A mirage is a trick of the light that

can happen when air near the ground is hotter than the air above.

The temperature difference 'bends' the path of the light so that

things seem to be in one place when they are really in another.

The traveller's pool of water is really a reflection of the sky!

3

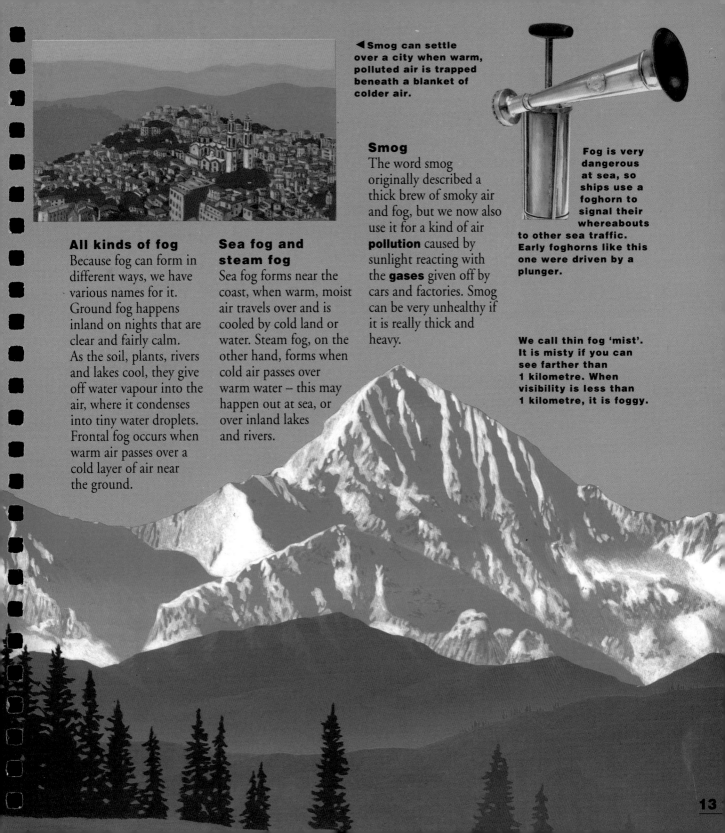

◀ Smog can settle over a city when warm, polluted air is trapped beneath a blanket of colder air.

Smog

The word smog originally described a thick brew of smoky air and fog, but we now also use it for a kind of air **pollution** caused by sunlight reacting with the **gases** given off by cars and factories. Smog can be very unhealthy if it is really thick and heavy.

Fog is very dangerous at sea, so ships use a foghorn to signal their whereabouts to other sea traffic. Early foghorns like this one were driven by a plunger.

We call thin fog 'mist'. It is misty if you can see farther than 1 kilometre. When visibility is less than 1 kilometre, it is foggy.

All kinds of fog

Because fog can form in different ways, we have various names for it. Ground fog happens inland on nights that are clear and fairly calm. As the soil, plants, rivers and lakes cool, they give off water vapour into the air, where it condenses into tiny water droplets. Frontal fog occurs when warm air passes over a cold layer of air near the ground.

Sea fog and steam fog

Sea fog forms near the coast, when warm, moist air travels over and is cooled by cold land or water. Steam fog, on the other hand, forms when cold air passes over warm water – this may happen out at sea, or over inland lakes and rivers.

Tricks of the light

1.+2. Haloes are misty circles around the Moon or Sun caused by light reflecting off ice crystals in high, thin clouds.

1

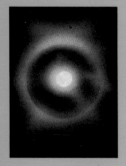

Deep in the desert, a thirsty traveller gasps to see a shimmering pool of water … but can he believe his eyes? A mirage is a trick of the light that can happen when air near the ground is hotter than the air above. The temperature difference 'bends' the path of the light so that things seem to be in one place when they are really in another. The traveller's pool of water is really a reflection of the sky!

3

► Auroras are spectacular curtains of red, green and yellow light, caused by electrically charged particles from the Sun colliding with the atmosphere.

5. As sunlight passes through a glass prism it splits into a rainbow, just as it does when it beams through raindrops. A second prism, and the rainbow changes back into white light. ◆

3. The Thompson twins of Tintin fame are tricked by a mirage in the desert!

4. The sky glows red even after the Sun sets because some light is reflected back to us by specks of dust and water in the air.

4

Refraction

Light travels in straight lines and cannot bend, although sometimes it appears to. When light travels through different materials – such as from cold air to hot, or from air into water – it changes speed. And when light changes speed, it alters direction slightly and seems to bend. This 'bending' is called refraction.

I can see a rainbow

Although sunlight looks colourless, the bright hues of a rainbow show that it is really made up of many colours. Rainbows form when sunlight passes through a veil of falling raindrops. Each drop refracts the light, splitting it into glowing shades of red, orange, yellow, green, blue, indigo and violet.

Spoon trick

You can see how light refracts when it passes from air into water if you put a spoon in a glass and then fill it with water (◆). The spoon will appear to bend.

▼ Although we can only see seven colours in a rainbow, there are more than 100 shades.

The front sweeps by, from left to right, with strong wind gusts and squalls of heavy rain.

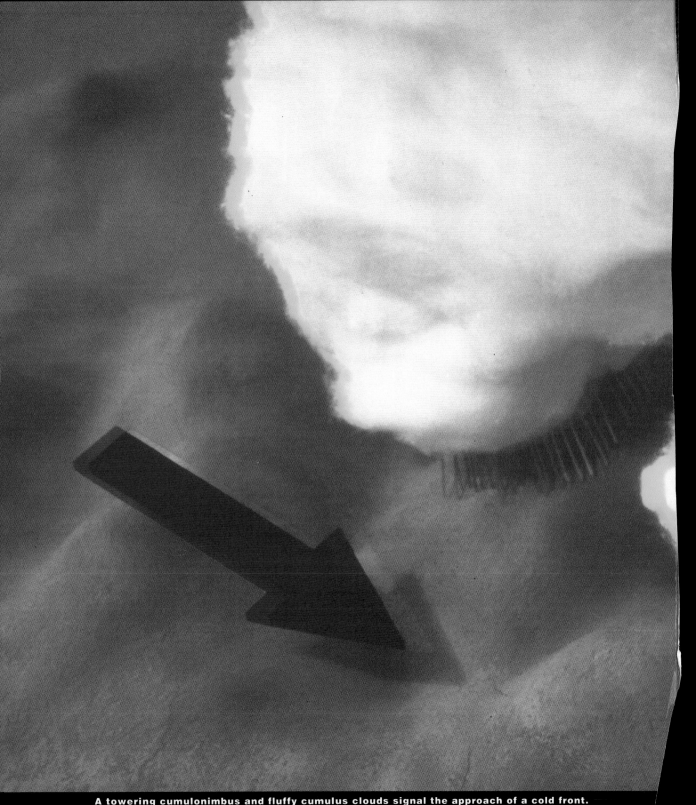

A towering cumulonimbus and fluffy cumulus clouds signal the approach of a cold front.

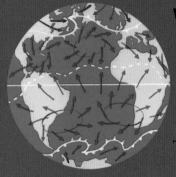

Unfold these pages to see weather fronts in 3-D.

Because the Earth spins, the great winds blow towards the right in the northern hemisphere, and to the left in the southern.

The weather is always changing, blown around the world by moving air – the wind. But what makes the wind blow? Wind is caused by differences in **air pressure** and temperature. Warm air is lighter than cool air, so it tends to rise. As it does, cold air moves in to take its place. At the same time, high-pressure air will flow to wherever the pressure is lower. The **poles** are colder than the **equator**, and the air pressure over them is higher – differences that give birth to the Earth's great wind systems.

Cumulus

Cumulonimbus

Cold air undercuts warm air

As the depression sweeps over the coast, a cold front brings high, icy cirrus clouds followed by:
1. Altocumulus
2. Cumulus
3. Cumulonimbus
4. A storm

Highs...
Anticyclones are slow-moving, high-pressure weather systems which usually bring clear skies and fine weather.

... and lows
Wind, rain and even snow are swept in by low-pressure weather systems known as **depressions**. Most depressions are born over the Atlantic and Pacific oceans, where the cold Arctic air mass meets the warmer and wetter, tropical air masses along a line called the polar **front**.

Life of a depression
On these two pages (moving from left to right) you can see how a depression shapes the weather. The warm, moist air of a warm front is forced upwards as it collides with a mass of heavier, colder air (below). As the warm air cools, its moisture **condenses** into clouds and then into heavy rain.

As the cold front moves in from the sea (page 16), cold air undercuts the warm air, forcing it up into lofty cumulonimbus storm clouds.

Warm air rising

Cold air

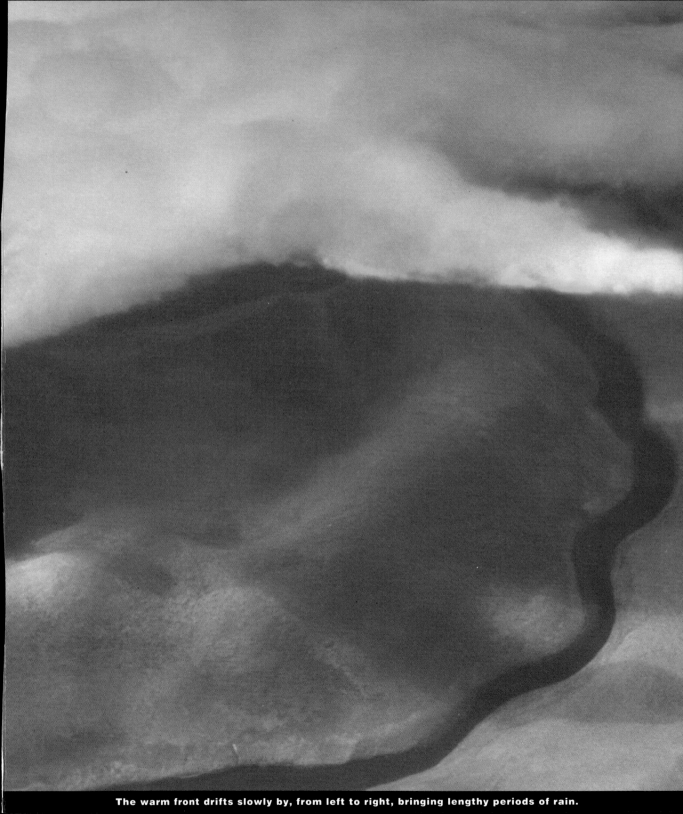

The warm front drifts slowly by, from left to right, bringing lengthy periods of rain.

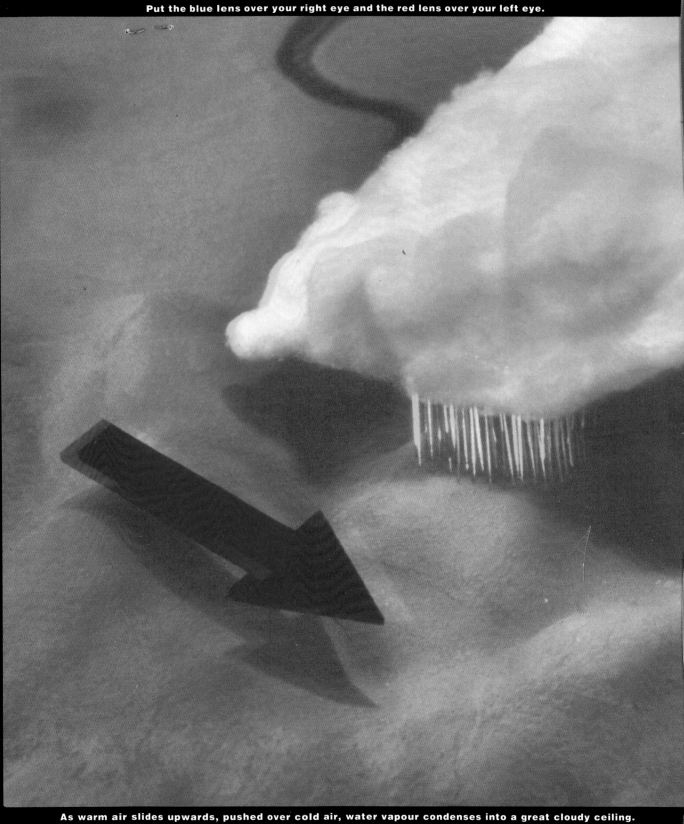

As warm air slides upwards, pushed over cold air, water vapour condenses into a great cloudy ceiling.

Blowing in the wind

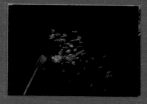

▲ **Wind helps plants by scattering their fruits and seeds.** ◆ **Some fruits have wings or hairy parachutes to help them fly.**

▲ **By day, air warmed over the land rises. Cool air from the sea pushes in beneath it as a cool sea breeze.**

▲ **At night, the land cools faster than the sea. Now breezes flow from land to sea.**

Three great wind systems surge over the face of the Earth. The fierce, chilly Polar Easterlies swirl around the North and South **poles**, while the warm Trade Winds blow steadily in the region above and below the **equator**. Between the Easterlies and the Trades beat the storm-bearing Westerlies. These great global winds shape the Earth's weather, but there are also smaller, local winds – created by high mountain ranges, for example, or by differences in temperature between land and sea, day and night. (You can find out more about local winds on pages 37–38.)

▲ **A medieval wind compass** ◆

▶ **When wind meets a mountain, it rises and cools. Its water vapour condenses to fall as rain. Sweeping down the far slope, the air gets drier and warmer. In the Swiss Alps, such warm winds are known as föhns. In the Rockies, they are called chinooks.**

Force 10 = Whole gale, winds 89-102 km/h, severe damage to trees and buildings

Force 11 = Storm, winds 103-117 km/h, widespread damage

Force 12 = Hurricane, winds over 117 km/h, devastation

Force 0 = Complete calm, wind less than 1 km/h, water like a mirror

Force 2 = Light breeze, winds 6-11 km/h, water rippled into wavelets

Force 3-4 = Gentle to moderate breeze, winds 12-28 km/h, flags blow out

Sir Francis Beaufort

Beaufort scale

In 1805, a British naval officer called Francis **Beaufort** introduced a scale (from 0 to 12) for measuring wind speed at sea. Beaufort developed the scale by matching the customs for setting a ship's sails with the speed and strength of the wind. He used everyday sailing terms for each level of his scale, and it is now used to describe the effect of each wind speed on the surface of the water, as well as on a range of everyday objects on land – from smoke to flags, trees and roof slates – in knots, miles per hour or kilometres per hour.

Force 5 = Fresh breeze, winds 29-38 km/h, moderate waves, many whitecaps

Force 7 = Moderate gale, winds 50-61 km/h, sea heaps up, white foam blown about

Whirling Winds

Whirlwinds, twisters, willy-willys – nature's most violent and destructive winds have many descriptive names. Tornadoes rarely measure more than 300 metres across. They form over land and usually last for only 15 to 20 minutes, but during this time they may race along faster than 100 kilometres per hour, ripping houses apart, uprooting trees and smashing cars – their winds spiralling at over 400 kilometres per hour. People and animals caught in their path may be killed by flying wreckage. Tornadoes begin deep inside vast cumulonimbus storm clouds which are growing so swiftly that they hoover up warm air with enough force to create a ferocious whirlpool of wind. Within minutes the wind snakes and spirals its way to the ground ... and a roaring, battering tornado is born!

▲ Weather planes fly into hurricanes to measure the speed, direction and strength of the wind. But no plane could ever survive a tornado.

▶ From northern Texas through to Kansas lies a belt of country known as 'tornado alley'. Hundreds of tornadoes come thundering through here every year. ◆◆

1. **Troposphere**
2. **Stratosphere**
3. **Mesosphere**
4. **Thermosphere**

4

3

2

1

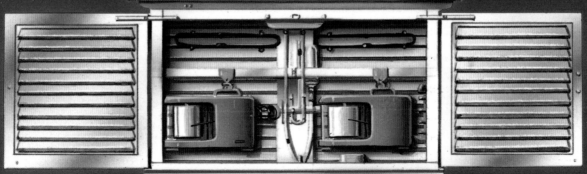

Land stations

Around the world, there are thousands of weather observation stations on land, where measurements are taken every 3 or 6 hours, day and night, and then forwarded to forecasting offices for analysis. Instruments are usually housed inside Stevenson screens, and include thermometers to measure maximum and minimum temperature, and a **hygrometer** for humidity. Rainfall is also measured. Wind speed and direction are recorded by an **anemometer**.

▲ Special weather research aircraft carry a range of sophisticated recording instruments.

Spies in the sky

Aircraft are used to record the weather in upper levels of the **troposphere**, while helium-filled weather balloons float high into the **stratosphere**. The balloons carry a packet of instruments called a radiosonde, to measure temperature, pressure and humidity of the upper air.

All at sea

Weather readings are also taken by ships and by weather buoys.

A Stevenson screen protects instruments from sun and rain. Its slatted sides allow the air to flow through.

The instruments bottom left and right continually record humidity and temperature, on slowly turning paper charts.

Forecasting the weather

▲ In a TV studio, the weather presenter is filmed in front of a blank screen. Satellite photos (below) and weather maps are added by the control room.

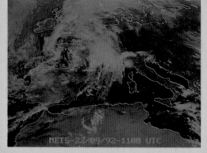

Only the most powerful supercomputers can handle all the data that is constantly being fed into central forecasting offices – to be useful in predicting the weather, they need to be capable of making millions of calculations a second. The computers supply information as sets of figures, which **meteorologists** use to draw up weather maps and to make daily forecasts. Finally, all the information is passed on to radio and television stations, and to newspapers. Forecasts are rarely 100 per cent accurate – rapid weather changes may bring surprises. But they give helpful warning of storms and cold spells, allowing ship and aircraft pilots to avoid bad weather, and farmers to plan when to plant and harvest their crops.

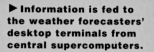

▶ Information is fed to the weather forecasters' desktop terminals from central supercomputers.

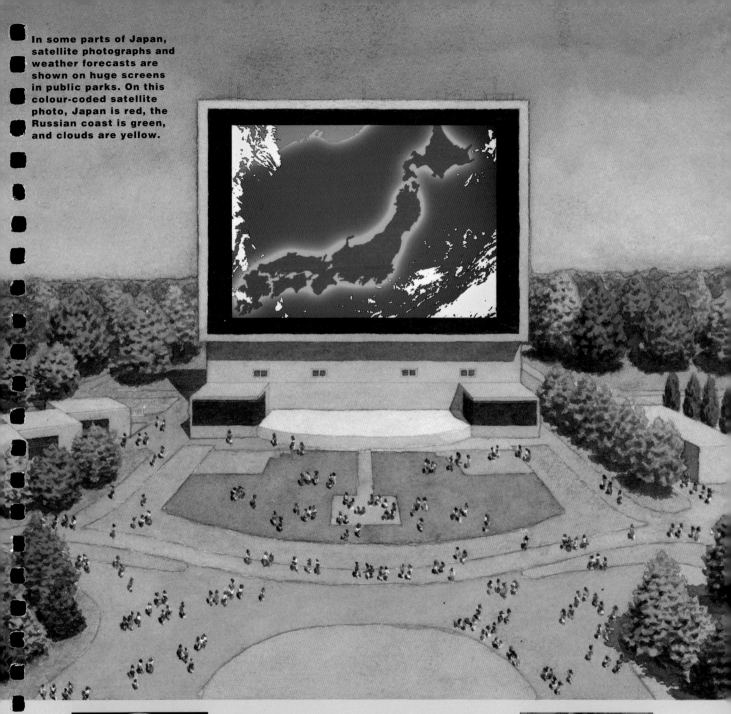

In some parts of Japan, satellite photographs and weather forecasts are shown on huge screens in public parks. On this colour-coded satellite photo, Japan is red, the Russian coast is green, and clouds are yellow.

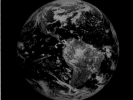

A satellite photograph shows the swirling cloud patterns that form the world's main weather systems at one moment in time.

A sequence of satellite photographs of cloud patterns gives clues as to how the weather will develop.

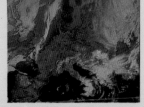

25

Weather patterns

Although in many places the weather can change from month to month, or even from day to day, it follows a certain pattern in every place on Earth. The Sahara Desert is usually hot and dry, for example, while the Amazon rainforest is hot and wet. The pattern of weather an area receives over months or years is its **climate**. It depends mainly on how close the area is to the **equator**, how far from the sea, and how high above **sea level**. And it is determined by measuring such things as temperature, rainfall and hours of sunshine. In many places the climate changes throughout the year – these changes are called seasons.

◀A sunshine recorder measures daily hours of sunshine. The glass ball focuses the Sun's rays so that they burn the strip of card mounted beneath it.

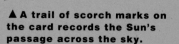

▲A trail of scorch marks on the card records the Sun's passage across the sky.

Tropical grassland – hot with 2 seasons (wet and dry)

Mountain – warm lower down; cold and snowy on peaks

Desert – hot and dry, very little rain

Cold forests – short, warm summers; long, snowy winter

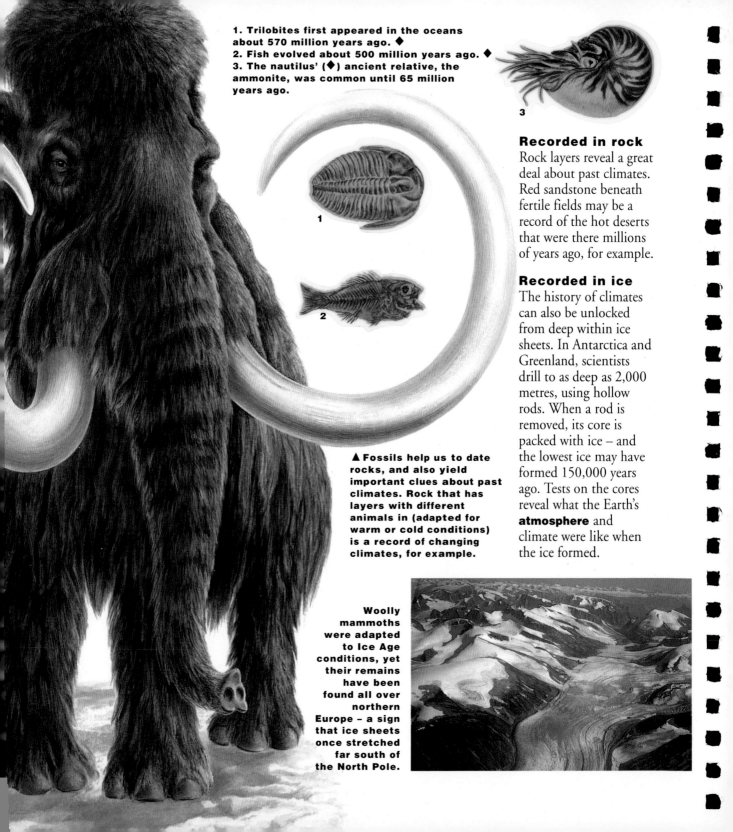

1. Trilobites first appeared in the oceans about 570 million years ago. ◆
2. Fish evolved about 500 million years ago. ◆
3. The nautilus' (◆) ancient relative, the ammonite, was common until 65 million years ago.

Recorded in rock

Rock layers reveal a great deal about past climates. Red sandstone beneath fertile fields may be a record of the hot deserts that were there millions of years ago, for example.

Recorded in ice

The history of climates can also be unlocked from deep within ice sheets. In Antarctica and Greenland, scientists drill to as deep as 2,000 metres, using hollow rods. When a rod is removed, its core is packed with ice – and the lowest ice may have formed 150,000 years ago. Tests on the cores reveal what the Earth's **atmosphere** and climate were like when the ice formed.

▲ Fossils help us to date rocks, and also yield important clues about past climates. Rock that has layers with different animals in (adapted for warm or cold conditions) is a record of changing climates, for example.

Woolly mammoths were adapted to Ice Age conditions, yet their remains have been found all over northern Europe – a sign that ice sheets once stretched far south of the North Pole.

Animals and plants
have adapted to survive
every climate. ◆◆◆◆◆◆
Animals that live in cold places
tend to have warm, furry coats and
thick layers of body fat, for example.

Mediterranean – hot, dry summer; mild, wet winter

Tropical forests – hot and wet, with rain throughout year

Polar – very cold all year round

Temperate – warm, wet summer; cool, wet winter

Changing climates

▼ As climates change, so do animals. Elephants are adapted for tropical climates – they do not need the woolly coat of their ancient relative, the mammoth.

▲ Taking an ice core

Climates have not always been the same as they are today – in the past 2 million years, the Earth experienced an **Ice Age**. During the coldest periods, ice sheets up to 3,000 metres thick spread from the **poles** to cover much of Europe, North America and Russia. Since the Ice Age ended about 10,000 years ago, climates have gradually become warmer. Because of **pollution** we may now be threatened by **global warming**.

If climates carry on getting warmer, more land will become barren desert, while polar ice will melt, flooding the coasts.

"Even the rainbow has a body

made of the drizzling rain

and is an architecture of

glistening atoms

built up, built up.

Yet you can't lay your

hand on it

nay, nor even your mind."

D H Lawrence
(1885–1930)
From 'The Rainbow'

◀ **An aurora borealis**

Amazing weather

The world's wettest place is Mawsynram, Meghalaya State, India. An average 11,873 mm of rain falls each year.

The world's driest place is the Pacific Coast of Chile, South America. The average annual rainfall is less than 0.1 mm.

The highest temperature ever recorded in the shade was taken at Al'Azīzīyah, Libya. On September 13, 1922, the temperature soared to a scorching 58 °C.

The coldest temperature ever recorded is −89.2 °C, taken in July 1983, at Vostok, Antarctica.

The world's windiest place is Commonwealth Bay, George V Coast, Antarctica, where gales frequently reach speeds of up to 320 km/h.

The most rapid
temperature change
occurred at Spearfish,
South Dakota, USA. At
7.30 am on January 23,
1943, the temperature
was −20 °C. By 7.32,
it had risen to 7 °C,
an incredible increase
of 27 °C in 2 minutes!

The heaviest hailstones
ever recorded weighed
almost 1 kilogram. They
killed 92 people in
Bangladesh in 1986.

The most damaging
hurricane was Hurricane
Andrew which, in August
1992, is estimated to
have caused some
US $22 billion worth of
damage.

One of the longest-lasting
rainbows occured over
Sheffield, England, on
March 14, 1994 – it
glowed for 6 hours.

The greatest loss of life
caused by a tornado
occurred in Bangladesh
in April 1989. About 1,300
people were killed.

Famous scientists and observers

Francis Beaufort

(1774–1857) Born in Ireland, Beaufort became an admiral in the British navy. In 1805, he introduced a system for recording wind speed at sea without the need for any equipment. The Beaufort Scale, as it became known, uses a scale of 0 to 12. Each number is linked to a description of the state of the sea and of a sailing ship's sails. The scale was later expanded to include descriptions of the effect of wind on land objects such as trees and buildings. The Beaufort Scale is still used today.

Joseph Black

(1728–1799) A Scottish **chemist** and professor of medicine, Black discovered **carbon dioxide** in the 1750s, although he called it 'fixed air'. He was the first person to realize that there are **gases** other than air, and the first to experiment with gases in a scientific way.

Robert Boyle

(1627–1691) Born in Ireland, Boyle lived in England for most of his life, studying philosophy and conducting scientific experiments in physics and **chemistry**. With his assistant Robert Hooke, Boyle discovered that something in air is essential both to animal life and to burning. Later scientists identified it as a **gas** and, in 1777, **Lavoisier** named it **oxygen**.

Galileo Galilei

(1564–1642) This famous Italian mathematician and astronomer was born in Pisa. Among many other achievements, Galileo invented the thermoscope (an early form of thermometer) in the 1590s. In 1609, he was one of the first people to use the newly invented telescope to study the night sky.

Jan Baptista van Helmont

(1579–1644) Born in Brussels, van Helmont was the first person to use the word **gas**. He discovered that there are different gases, but he had no way of studying them scientifically.

Luke Howard

(1772–1864) A pharmacist who was fascinated by the weather, Howard worked out the system that **meteorologists** still use today for naming different kinds of cloud. By observing the shapes and heights of clouds, he saw that they could be divided into three basic families – puffy clouds (which he named cumulus), layered clouds (stratus) and wispy clouds (cirrus). There are four kinds of cloud in the cumulus family, and three each in the stratus and cirrus families. Every shape, colour or size of cloud can be identified as one of these ten types.

Antoine Laurent Lavoisier

(1743–1794) This great French scientist developed the work of **Priestley** and **Scheele** in a series of experiments in the 1770s. Having proved that air is a mix of gases, Lavoisier went on to show that, when a substance burns, it combines with something in the air – a gas which he named **oxygen**. Lavoisier was executed on the guillotine in 1794.

Blaise Pascal

(1623–1662) A brilliant French mathematician and scientist, Pascal did not go to school. Instead, his father taught him ancient languages at home and refused to teach him any science – until Pascal revealed, at the age of 11, that he had secretly taught himself geometry! Son and father later worked together on various experiments to confirm **Torricelli**'s theory on **air pressure**. In 1648, Pascal (who was in poor health and had a great fear of heights) persuaded his brother-in-law to repeat Torricelli's **barometer** experiment on the summit of the Puy de Dôme mountain.

The results proved that air pressure reduces with height. In 1654, Pascal gave up science and became a monk.

Joseph Priestley

(1733–1804) This English clergyman and scientist studied electricity before taking up **chemistry** in the late 1760s. At that time, only three **gases** were known – air (not then known to be a mix of gases), **carbon dioxide** and hydrogen. Priestley discovered another ten, including laughing gas (nitrous oxide)! One of these gases, which he observed made a lighted candle burn more brightly and did not kill his laboratory mice, he named 'dephlogisticated air'. He repeated his experiment in 1774 in Paris for **Lavoisier**, who grasped the importance of this new gas, and later named it **oxygen**.

Lewis Fry Richardson

(1881–1953) This English **meteorologist** and teacher was the first person to try to predict the weather using mathematical calculations. His approach gave later meteorologists the basics for working out weather forecasts by using computers to carry out calculations accurately and quickly enough for forecasts to be useful.

Carl Wilhelm Scheele

(1742–1786) A Swedish **chemist**. By 1772 Scheele had found that air contains a substance which encourages burning. He called it 'fire air'. He passed information about his experiments to **Lavoisier** who, also drawing on **Priestley**'s discovery, named the substance **oxygen**. Among many other important achievements, Scheele also discovered chlorine.

Evangelista Torricelli

(1608–1647) This Italian mathematician and scientist worked for a few months as **Galileo**'s assistant. In 1644, he described in a letter how **air pressure** could be measured by a **barometer**.

Invented in 1757, the sextant helped sailors to fix their position at sea.

Local winds

Bora

A bitingly cold wind that affects northern Italy and the east coast of the Adriatic Sea.

Brickfielder

A hot and dusty wind in southeastern Australia which blows from the desert in summer.

Chinook

A dry, warm, westerly wind in the eastern foothills of the US and Canadian Rockies, which speeds up the thaw of winter snow. Named after a local Indian tribe.

Etesian

Dry northerly winds which blow continuously from mid-May to mid-October in the eastern Mediterranean and Aegean seas.

Föhn

A dry, warm wind which blows down some Alpine valleys. Like the **chinook**, it can speed up the spring thaw. But the föhn is also blamed for causing headaches, heart attacks and feelings of deep sadness.

Haboob

A hot, gusty wind in the Sudan, in northeast Africa, which often brings a sandstorm.

Harmattan

A dry hot wind from the Sahara Desert which blows over the countries of West Africa, bringing dust storms.

Mistral

A strong, cold, dry wind from the north which often funnels down the Rhône valley, in the south of France. Its sharp chill makes an unwelcome change to the normally warm Mediterranean weather. Farmers hate the mistral because it damages their crops – they fight it by planting hedges of trees around their fields and orchards to act as windbreaks.

Monsoon

A seasonal wind in India and several other tropical countries. For half the year, the monsoon blows from the southwest, usually bringing heavy rain. At the end of the monsoon season, the wind changes and blows from the northeast, bringing cool, dry weather. Monsoon rains are needed to make food crops grow, but they sometimes cause serious flooding.

Santa Ana

An uncomfortably hot, dry, dusty wind in southern California. It blows from the high inland desert, funnelling down through narrow mountain canyons to the coastal plain.

Sirocco

A hot wind which blows northwards from the Sahara Desert. As the sirocco crosses the Mediterranean, it picks up a lot of water **vapour**. This means that it is very humid by the time it reaches Italy and other countries on the southern shores of Europe, where it can damage crops.

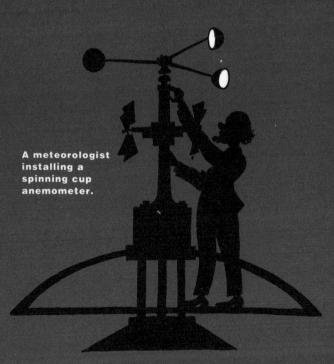

A meteorologist installing a spinning cup anemometer.

Useful words

Acid rain

Poisonous **gases** such as sulphur dioxide and nitrogen dioxide are given off when some fuels are burned. When these gases are dissolved by water droplets in clouds, they form a weak acid. And when this acid falls to the ground as rain or snow, it harms the water and the land.

Air pressure

Even though we do not feel it, air has weight and is pushing down on us all the time. Air pressure is caused by the weight of the atmosphere pressing down on the Earth. This pressure varies, depending on weather conditions and the height of the land above **sea level**. Areas of high air pressure are called **anticyclones**, and areas of low pressure are called cyclones or **depressions**.

Anemometer

An instrument for measuring wind speed and direction. Most weather stations use the spinning cup anemometer, invented in 1846 by the Irish astronomer Thomas Robinson. (See picture on page 38.)

Anticyclone

An area of high **air pressure**. Anticyclones often cover large areas (around 1,500 kilometres across) and bring settled, dry, cold or sunny weather.

Atmosphere

The layer of **gases** around a planet. The Earth's atmosphere is mainly made up of nitrogen (78%) and **oxygen** (21%), plus small amounts of **carbon dioxide** (0.03 %) and other gases, including water **vapour**. It also contains particles of salt, dust and dirt. All nine planets in the solar system have atmospheres, but only the Earth's contains plenty of oxygen, the gas every animal needs to breathe to stay alive.

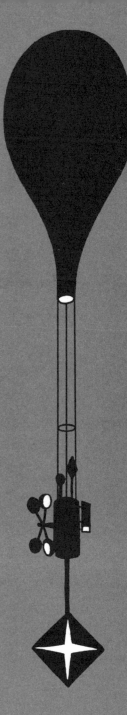

A weather balloon

Barometer

An instrument that measures **air pressure**. By noting changes in air pressure, people can use barometers to help forecast the weather. A high pressure reading signals settled, dry weather, while a low one means that unsettled, wet or stormy weather is on the way.

Billion

One thousand million (1,000,000,000).

Carbon dioxide

One of the **gases** found in small amounts in the air. Plants use carbon dioxide to make food in their leaves, through a process called photosynthesis, and they give off **oxygen**. Animals do the opposite, taking in oxygen and breathing out carbon dioxide. Certain kinds of fuel also give off carbon dioxide when burned (see **Pollution**).

Chemist

A scientist who studies substances – what they are like, how they behave, how they are affected by temperature and pressure, and how they react with other substances.

Climate

The typical pattern of weather usually found in an area (including the temperature, hours of sunshine, rainfall and wind conditions) measured over a long period of time, usually at least 50 years.

Condense

If a **gas** or a **vapour** cools to a low enough temperature, it changes into a liquid. This process is known as condensation. Fog and clouds form when air that contains a lot of water vapour cools, and the vapour condenses into tiny water droplets. If the water droplets become large and heavy enough, they fall as rain.

Depression

An area of low **air pressure**, also known as a cyclone. Depressions often bring windy, wet and unsettled weather.

Equator

An imaginary line around the Earth, halfway between the North and South **poles**. The equator divides the Earth into two equal parts called hemispheres.

Front

The area where one mass of air meets another mass of air of a different temperature. Television and newspaper weather charts frequently show the position of cold or warm fronts. The arrival of a front means a change in the weather.

Gas

One of the three forms in which materials exist. The other two forms are solids and liquids. Solids, such as ice, have a definite shape and have to be forced to take a new one. Liquids, such as water, can change shape and flow. Gases, such as those in the air, have no fixed shape and can move around freely. A gas can expand (get bigger) and fill up any container.

Global warming

A gradual rise in the temperature of the Earth's surface and its **atmosphere**, which may be due to the **greenhouse effect**.

Greenhouse effect

Greenhouses are warm because their glass panes let sunlight through, but stop warmth in the sunlight from escaping. **Carbon dioxide** and other **gases** in the Earth's **atmosphere** act in a similar way to greenhouse glass. They let the Sun's rays through, but stop most of the heat given off by the Earth from escaping back into space. The greenhouse gases are essential – nights would be freezing cold without them. However, in the past 100 or so years, **pollution** has resulted in a steady increase in the greenhouse gases in the atmosphere, and the Earth has been getting warmer. Many scientists think that if the greenhouse effect continues to increase at its present rate, the **polar** ice caps may melt, causing seas to rise and flooding coastal land.

Hygrometer

An instrument for measuring humidity (the amount of water in the air). Most of the water in air takes the form of water **vapour**. The amount of vapour the air can hold depends on temperature – hot air can be very humid (with a lot of water vapour), but in cool air the vapour **condenses** into rain or fog. So, depending on temperature, a rise in humidity may be a sign that rain is on the way.

Mercury

A silvery metal, the only one to stay liquid at room temperature. It is widely used in **barometers** and thermometers.

Mesosphere

The layer of the **atmosphere** above the **stratosphere** and below the **thermosphere**, which stretches from about 50 kilometres to about 80 kilometres above the Earth's surface.

Meteorologist

A scientist who studies the atmosphere, and weather and **climate**. The word *meteor* comes from the Greek for 'something high up'.

Oxygen

A **gas** that forms 21% of the air around us. All animals breathe oxygen and could not live without it. Oxygen is also needed for burning – when things burn, they combine with oxygen in the air. Oxygen was discovered by Carl Wilhem **Scheele** and Joseph **Priestley**, and named by Antoine **Lavoisier** in 1777.

Ozone

Ozone is a form of **oxygen**. In liquid form it is used as a powerful germ-killer and bleach. A layer of ozone **gas** is also found in the **stratosphere**, at between 15 and 30 kilometres above the Earth's surface. This ozone layer absorbs most of the ultraviolet light rays

Winter   Spring   Summer   Autumn

from the Sun – harmful rays which would burn us if they got through. A small amount of ultraviolet does reach the **troposphere**, which is why people can suffer from sunburn. In recent years, scientists have discovered a thinning in the ozone layer, over the **poles** every spring. Many people believe that this has resulted from **pollution** of the atmosphere by gases known as CFCs, used in aerosols and fridges.

Poles

The Earth has an imaginary line running through its centre – the axis around which it spins. The two places at either end of the axis are called the geographic poles – the North Pole, in the middle of the Arctic Circle, and the South Pole, in the middle of the Antarctic Circle.

Pollution

Pollution is the spoiling or dirtying of air, water or land by the addition of something harmful to human, animal or plant life. The air in many big cities is polluted by the **gases** produced by the engines of cars and other machinery. Fuels such as petrol, coal and natural gas give off **carbon dioxide** and other gases when burned. In this century, people have used much more of this kind of fuel. This has increased the amount of carbon dioxide gas in the Earth's **atmosphere** and could lead to **global warming**. (*See also* **Acid rain**, **Greenhouse effect**.)

Sea level

The point from which the height of the land is measured. Sea level is the average surface of the sea at the halfway point between high and low tides.

Stratosphere

The second layer of the **atmosphere**, above the **troposphere**, which rises to about 50 kilometres above the Earth's surface. It is very cold – below freezing point in all but the highest part. There are hardly any clouds and little wind in stratosphere, which is why aircraft usually fly this high. It also contains the **ozone** layer.

Thermosphere

The fourth layer of the **atmosphere**, which begins at around 80 kilometres above the Earth's surface. There is very little air at this height. Weather satellites are stationed in the thermosphere. Beyond the thermosphere is the exosphere, where the air is so thin that it merges into space.

Troposphere

The lowest layer of the Earth's **atmosphere**. This is the air we breathe, and it contains most of the **oxygen** in the atmosphere. It is also where most clouds form and nearly all the weather changes take place. The troposphere is about 16 kilometres thick over the **equator**, and about 10 kilometres thick over the **poles**.

Vapour

A vapour is a **gas** that can easily change back into a liquid. Air contains water vapour. If air cools down, the vapour **condenses** and changes back into water droplets.

Index

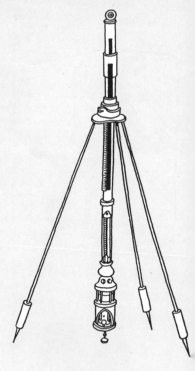

Bold numerals indicate insert pages

Time line

	Ancient World	Middle Ages 476-1492	Renaissance 1492-1600
Weather	**c. 10,000, years ago** End of Ice Age **c. 1,300 BC** First weather observations written down, in China **c. 350 BC** Rain gauge first used, in India **c. 340 BC** Aristotle wrote *Meteorolgica*, the first book about the atmosphere		**1590s** Galileo invented the thermoscope, an early kind of thermometer
Science and Nature	**c. 1.8 million years ago** First stone tools used **c. 1 million years ago** Fire first used **c. 4000 BC** First metal objects made **c. 3000 BC** Wheels first used **200s BC** Aristarchus suggested that the Earth orbits the Sun	**c. 500** Mathematicians in India invented zero and decimal numbers **868** First complete book printed in China **c. 1000s** The Chinese used black powder (gunpowder) in firework rockets **c. 1440** Gutenberg started to use his printing press	**c. 1490s** Leonardo da Vinci designed flying machines **1543** Copernicus published his opinion that the Earth moves around the Sun **1543** Vesalius published first accurate descriptions of the human body **1590s** Microscope invented
Visual Arts	**c. 30,000 BC** Earliest sculptures made **c. 15,000 BC** Cave paintings at Lascaux, France **c. 2500 BC** The Great Pyramid built at Giza, Egypt **1300 BC** Chinese produced glazed pottery **c. 150 BC** *Venus de Milo*	**c. 800** *Book of Kells*, illuminated manuscript made in Ireland **c. 1230** Gothic cathedral of Chartres completed, France **c. 1304-1313** Giotto decorated Arena Chapel in Italy with frescoes **1409** Donatello's *David*	**c. 1495-1497** Leonardo da Vinci's *The Last Supper* **1503-1593** St Peter's built in Rome, Italy **1508-1512** Michelangelo painted the ceiling of the Sistine Chapel **1513** Dürer's engraving *St Jerome in his Study* **c. 1554** Cellini's *Perseus*
Performing Arts	**60,000 BC** The first flutes were made out of bone **900s BC** Indian temple rituals embrace dance drama **c. 534 BC** Earliest reference to competition for tragedies, in Ancient Greece	**700s** Japanese court music (gagaku) developed **740** First Chinese drama school founded **1100s** Troubadours told of heroes and legends in song **c. 1300s** Mystery play cycles emerge in Europe **c. 1370** Emergence of Nō theatre in Japan	**1500s** Musical scales were developed **c. 1545** Earliest record of commedia dell'arte **1567** The first English public theatre opened, in London **1581** One of the first ballets performed, in France **c. 1595** Shakespeare's *Romeo and Juliet*
Literature	**c. 3500 BC** Writing was invented **1000 BC** Oldest books of the Old Testament put into writing **1000 BC** The *Rig-Veda* was composed in India **c. 700s BC** The *Iliad* and the *Odyssey* written	**c. 700s** *Beowulf* **1321** Dante's *Divine Comedy* **c. 1377** Langland's *The Vision of Piers Plowman* **1386-1400** Chaucer's *Canterbury Tales*	**1513** Machiavelli's *The Prince* **1590-1596** Spenser's *The Faerie Queene*

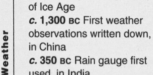

17th Century	18th Century	19th Century	20th Century

17th Century

1644 Torricelli described the first practical barometer
1667 Hooke invented the anemometer
1664 Folli invented the hygrometer

1609 Galileo made important astronomical observations with his telescope
1657 First pendulum clock made by Huygens
1687 Newton published his findings on gravity
1696 Thomas Savery invented the steam pump

1600 Caravaggio's *Calling of St Matthew*
1642 Rembrandt's *The Night Watch*
1656 Velázquez's *Las Meninas*
1668-1686 Palace of Versailles, France, built

1600s The first Stradivarius violins were made
1606 Ben Jonson's *Volpone*
1637 First public opera house opened, in Venice
1666 Molière's *The Misanthrope*

1605 Cervantes' *Don Quixote*
1667 Milton's *Paradise Lost* published
1678 Bunyan's *Pilgrim's Progress*

18th Century

1714 Fahrenheit invented the mercury thermometer, and a temperature scale
1742 Celsius devised the centigrade temperature scale
1777 Lavoisier named the gas oxygen

1749 Linnaeus introduced his binomial classification system for plants
1783 Montgolfier brothers launched hot-air balloon
1796 Jenner pioneered vaccination

1767-1744
Royal Crescent, Bath, England, constructed
1793 J.L. David's *Death of Marat*

1700 Congreve's *The Way of the World*
1725 Vivaldi's *The Four Seasons*
1729 J S Bach's *St Matthew Passion*
1741 Handel's *Messiah*
1764 Mozart composed his first symphony
c. 1773 Goethe began *Faust*

1719 Defoe's *Robinson Crusoe*
1726 Swift's *Gulliver's Travels*
1755 Dr Johnson published a dictionary of the English language

19th Century

1803 Howard grouped and named clouds
1805 Beaufort scale introduced
1846 Spinning cup anemometer invented
1854 UK Met Office formed
1898 First automated weather balloons launched

1800 Alessandro Volta invented the battery
1804 Trevithick built the first steam locomotive
1827 Niepce invented the photograph
1876 First telephone
1885 Benz built the first petrol-engine car

1820-1840s Hokusai's woodblock prints, Japan
1839 Turner's *Fighting Téméraire*
1851 Paxton's Crystal Palace erected in London
1872 Monet's *Impression: Sunrise*
1880 Rodin's *The Thinker*
1888 Van Gogh's *Sunflowers*

1808 Beethoven's *6th Symphony (Pastoral)*
1871 Verdi's opera *Aida*
1877 Tchaikovsky's ballet *Swan Lake*
1879 Ibsen's *A Doll's House*
1895 First regular public film shows, in Paris

1812 Grimm's Fairytales
1847 Charlotte Brontë's *Jane Eyre*
1849 Dickens began *David Copperfield*
1850 Wordsworth's *Prelude* published
1865 *Alice's Adventures in Wonderland* by Lewis Carroll

20th Century

1922 First weather bulletin broadcast on radio
1960 First weather satellite, TIROS 1, launched
1976 Viking spacecraft send back first weather reports from Mars

1903 Wright brothers flew the first powered aircraft
1905 Einstein published his theory of special relativity
1928 Discovery of penicillin
1936 First live, high-definition television service
1961 Yuri Gagarin was the first human in space
1971 Silicon chip invented

1907 Picasso's *Les Demoiselles d'Avignon*, the first cubist painting
1910 Matisse's *The Dance*
1935-36 Henry Moore's *Reclining Figure*
1962 Warhol's *One Hundred Campbell's Soup Cans*
1967 Bridget Riley's *Current*

c. 1900 Beginning of jazz
1901 Chekhov's *The Three Sisters* first performed
1909 Diaghilev presented his *Ballet Russes* in Paris
1927 First successful talkie, *The Jazz Singer*, released
1945 Britten's *Peter Grimes*
1954 Start of rock-'n'-roll

1913 D.H. Lawrence's *Sons and Lovers*
1922 James Joyce's *Ulysses* published
1927 Virginia Woolf's *To The Lighthouse*
1955 Patrick White's *The Tree of Man*

45

KINGFISHER
An imprint of Larousse plc
Elsley House, 24-30 Great Titchfield Street,
London W1P 7AD

Originally published in France by Editions Gallimard
Jeunesse under the title *Vents et nuages, le temps qu'il fait*

A CIP catalogue record for this book is available from
the British Library.

ISBN 1 85697 343 3

Typeset by SPAN, Lingfield, Surrey
Printed in Italy by Editoriale Libraria

Created by Pierre Marchand
French editorial and design team Diane Costa de
Beauregard, Catherine Bon de Sairigné, Isabelle Guillard,
David Alazraki, Pascal Hubert, Sarbacane, Raymond
Stoffel, Anne de Bouchony
French editorial advisers René Chaboud, Jean-Pierre
Verdet, Astronomer at the Paris Observatory
English translation, editorial and design team
Brigid Avison, Jackie Gaff, Christopher Maynard,
Terry Woodley

**Have you found the right place
for the stickers?**
Page 2 – **7**; Pages 4-5 – **14, 15**; Page
5 – **17**; Pages 14-15 – **26**; Page 15 – **19**;
Page 18 – **2, 3**; Page 20 – **20, 21**; Page
22 – **16, 18, 22**; Page 26 – **8, 9, 12, 13**;
Page 27 – **6, 10, 11, 23, 24, 25**; Page 28
– **1, 4, 5**.

Key

l = left	*b* = bottom
r = right	*m* = middle
t = top	*c* = column

Illustrators

Philippe Biard 24, 25; Christian
Broutin *cover*, 8, 9 and 9
(foldout), 18, 19 *(foldout recto
and verso)*; Jean-Philippe
Chabot *(foldout verso)*, 5*tr*, 26*br*;
Luc Favreau 7; Ute Fuhr/Raoul
Sautai 28*l*, 28*t*, 29*r*; Henri
Galeron 12, 13, 26*t*, 27 *(foldout
verso)*; Donald Grant 11, 10/11
(photo), 14, 15 *(photo)*, 20, 20
(die-cut insert recto), 22, 23,
26*b*, 29*tl*; Raymond Hermange
2, 3; Jacques Lerouge *(inside
cover and appendices)*; François
Place *sticker* 18*tr*; Jean-Marie
Poissenot 4, 4*bl (foldout insert)*,
4*m*, 5*mr*, 5*bl (foldout insert)*,
5*mb*, 5*tr*; Amato Soro 21*l*, 21
(die-cut insert); Pierre-Marie
Valat 16, 17.

Credits

Daniel Barthélémy/Bios, Paris 27
(foldout verso); Bibliothèque
central du Museum national
d'Histoire naturelle, Paris 5
(insert tr); Vincent Bretagnolle/

Bios, Paris 27 *(foldout recto br)*;
Clémentel, *Claude Monet
standing* , Musée d'Orsay/
Réunion des Musées Nationaux,
Paris 6*bl*; Denis-Huot, Bios,
Paris 27*bl*, 29*bl*; Jack Finch/
S.P.L./Cosmos, Paris *(cover
bm)*, 15*t*; Caspar David
Friedrich, *Traveller in a Sea of
Clouds*, Kunsthalle, Hamburg.
Bridgeman/Giraudon, Vanves 8;
Giraudon, Vanves *(cover br)*,
18*tr (liber floridus*, c. 1448 by
Lambert, Flanders, in the Musée
de Condé, Chantilly, France;
Hergé, *Tintin in the Land of
Black Gold*, publ. Casterman
14*mr*; Hiroshige, *Rainstorm at

Sono*, Musée Guimet/Réunion
des Musées Nationaux, Paris
10*tl*; Johnson Space Center
Houston, Texas/ NASA,
Washington 21*mr*; Patrick
Léger/Gallimard Jeunesse 5*l*,
13*tr*; Georges Lopez/Bios, Paris
27 *(foldout verso)*; Francisco
Marquez/Bios, Paris 27 *(foldout
verso bl)*; Météo France, Paris
(cover bl), 24*ml*, 25*bl*, 25*br*;
Claude Monet, *Les Meules fin
de l'été, Giverny*, 1891, Musée
d'Orsay/Réunion des Musées
Nationaux 6*tr*, *Meules, milieu du
jour*, 1890, Australian National
Gallery, Canberra 6*mr*, *Les
Meules à Giverny soleil
couchant*, 1889, Museum of
Modern Art, Saitama, Japan 6*br*;
Dr Norman Myers/Bruce
Coleman Ltd, Uxbridge, England
27*mr*; Nasa, Washington 2*tl*, 3*b*;
Pekka Parvianen/S.P.L./
Cosmos, Paris 30; S. Pearce,
Sir Francis Beaufort, 1850,
National Portrait Gallery, London
19*tl*; Eckart Pott/Bruce Coleman
Ltd, Uxbridge, England 27*br*;
Quesnel, *Pascal*, 17th Century,
Château de Versailles, Lauros/
Giraudon, Vanves 5 *(insert
recto tl)*; S.P.L./Cosmos, Paris
25*m*; Patrice Tourenne, Paris
10*br*; Valentin/Hoa Qui, Paris
10*tr*; Van Gogh, *Starry Night*,
1888, Musée d'Orsay/Réunion
des Musées Nationaux, Paris 2*tr*;
Albert Visage, Chateaurenard,
France 10; John Waters/Bruce
Coleman Ltd, Uxbridge, England
27*tl*; Jonathan Watts/S.P.L./
Cosmos, Paris 18*tl*.

Acknowledgements
Météo France, Paris; Constance
Moore, NASA; Alexandra Rose,
iconographer, New York; Carla
Wallace Noaa.